BEN FRANKLIN
HIS WIT AND WISDOM FROM A–Z

BY ALAN SCHROEDER

ILLUSTRATED BY
JOHN O'BRIEN

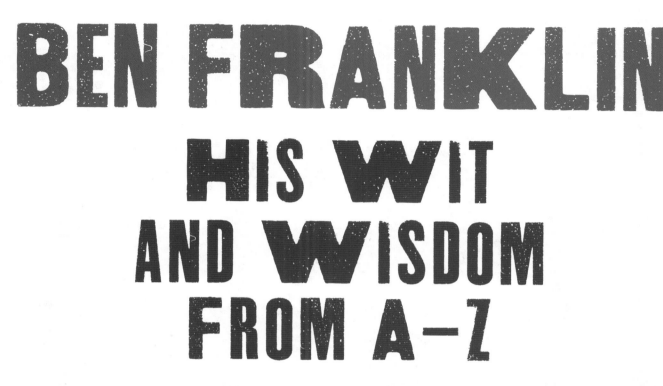

Holiday House / New York

A is for *Almanac*

Almanacs were very popular in colonial America. Every household had one. They sold well because they were full of useful information. Farmers relied on them to find out the best time of year to plant a particular crop. Sailors used them to study the rise and fall of the tides. Almanacs also contained calendars, weather forecasts, recipes, and medical advice.

Benjamin Franklin wrote and published the most popular almanac of all. It was called *Poor Richard's Almanack*, and every year he'd print a new edition.

Poor Richard's was full of clever sayings. People still enjoy reading them today.

Abiah – Abiah Folger was Benjamin Franklin's mother. She was twenty-two when she married Josiah Franklin, Ben's father. She and Josiah had ten children together.

WET PAINT

Wise men don't need advice.
Fools won't take it.

Never leave that till tomorrow which you can do today.

Apprentice – When Ben was twelve, he became an apprentice in his brother's printing shop. But he and James didn't get along.

Armonica – Ben Franklin invented a musical instrument called the armonica, which consisted of thirty-seven different-sized glass bowls. Once the tuned bowls had been set into motion, a person could play them simply by touching the spinning rims with a wet finger. The music produced was both sweet and haunting, and for a time the armonica was very popular. Mozart and Beethoven composed music for it.

B is for *Boston*

Benjamin Franklin was born in Boston, Massachusetts, in 1706 and lived there until he was seventeen. Boston was one of the largest cities in colonial America.

Bifocals – Ben invented bifocal eyeglasses. They allow people who wear glasses to see both close-up and far away.

Balloon – When Ben was elderly, he witnessed one of the first hot-air balloon ascensions. It took place in France in 1783. Ben and his grandson Benny cheered as the balloon took off.

Either write something worth reading or do things worth the writing.

The Constitution only gives people the right to pursue happiness. You have to catch it yourself.

C is for *Constitution*

Ben Franklin was a delegate to the Constitutional Convention, which met in Philadelphia in 1787. The delegates' job: to produce a lasting form of government for their country. The result of their work was the United States Constitution. As he looked over the finished document, Ben thought it had a few faults, but he urged everyone to sign it, "because I think a general government necessary for us."

Our new Constitution is now established, and has an appearance that promises permanency; but in the world nothing can be said to be certain except death and taxes.

Contract – As an apprentice, twelve-year-old Ben had to sign a contract, promising he would work for his brother for nine years. But he lasted only five.

Chess – Ben loved to play chess. Sometimes, he'd get so caught up in a game, he would play all night!

Games lubricate the mind.

D is for *Deborah*

Deborah Read was Benjamin Franklin's wife. They were married on September 1, 1730. Like many women in the colonies, Debbie could barely read or write. Nevertheless, she was of great help to Ben. She kept house, raised the children, and for many years worked with her husband in their general store. "She [was] a good and faithful helpmate," Ben later said of his wife.

Deborah died in 1774.

Declaration of Independence – On August 2, 1776, Benjamin Franklin signed the Declaration of Independence. It was one of the proudest days of his life.

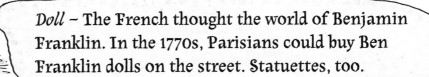

Doll – The French thought the world of Benjamin Franklin. In the 1770s, Parisians could buy Ben Franklin dolls on the street. Statuettes, too.

Duet – Ben loved music. Often, he and his daughter, Sally, would play duets together – Ben on the armonica, Sally on the harpsichord.

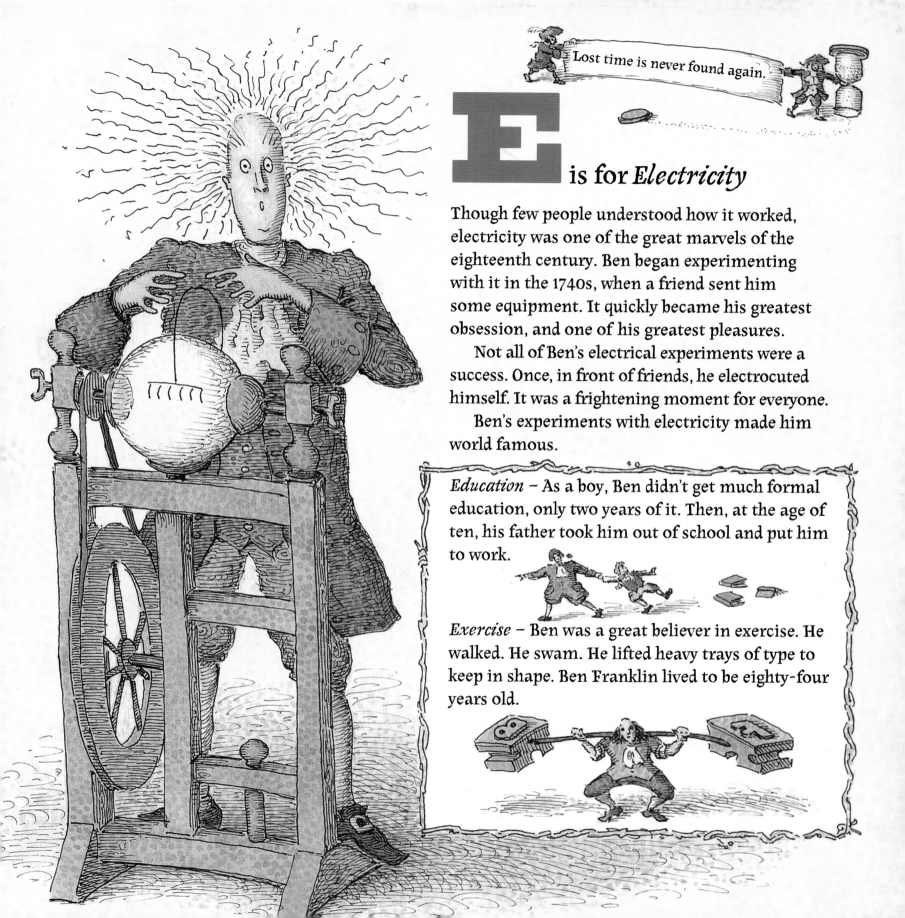

E is for *Electricity*

Though few people understood how it worked, electricity was one of the great marvels of the eighteenth century. Ben began experimenting with it in the 1740s, when a friend sent him some equipment. It quickly became his greatest obsession, and one of his greatest pleasures.

Not all of Ben's electrical experiments were a success. Once, in front of friends, he electrocuted himself. It was a frightening moment for everyone.

Ben's experiments with electricity made him world famous.

Education – As a boy, Ben didn't get much formal education, only two years of it. Then, at the age of ten, his father took him out of school and put him to work.

Exercise – Ben was a great believer in exercise. He walked. He swam. He lifted heavy trays of type to keep in shape. Ben Franklin lived to be eighty-four years old.

F is for *Franklin stove*

One of Ben's most successful inventions was a new type of stove, one that used less wood and gave off considerably more heat. He called it the "Pennsylvania fireplace," but the public gave it a new name: the "Franklin stove." Thousands were sold. Even Thomas Jefferson bought one to heat his home.

Save and have.

Every little . . .

makes a mickle.

Fishing – When Ben was a boy, fishing was one of his favorite pastimes.

1732   1736

Francis – One of Ben's sons. Franky was a bright and lively boy who died at the age of four from smallpox. Losing Francis was one of the great tragedies of Ben's life.

Frugal – Ben believed it was important to be frugal, to not waste money on foolish things.

G is for *General*

When Ben was fifty, he served briefly as a general in the army during the French and Indian War. He helped the British beat back the French, who were trying to move into the colonies. The British won, and back home Ben was given a hero's welcome.

George – Ben Franklin was living in London in 1760 when George III became king of England. Ben predicted he would have a "glorious" reign, but it wasn't meant to be. Starting in 1765 with the Stamp Act, George III began levying taxes on the colonies, one after another. Finally, the colonists rebelled, and in 1776 they fired off an eye-opening document to King George: the Declaration of Independence.

Kings and bears often worry their masters.

Gout – In his old age, Ben suffered from gout, a painful swelling of the joints. Gout made it difficult for him to get around.

ENGLAND

Well done is better than well said.

H is for *Hospital*

Ben did everything he could to make Philadelphia a better place.

When a friend complained that the city didn't have a hospital, Ben wrote about the problem in his newspaper. That got people talking. Then he asked friends and acquaintances for donations. Finally, he convinced the government to chip in, too.

Thanks to Ben Franklin, Philadelphia got its hospital.

Hardening off – When Ben was a baby, his mother dunked him in cold water three times a day. Babies were dunked all the time in colonial America. "Hardening off" was thought to keep infants healthy.

Hero – When Ben was seventeen, he saved a man from drowning.

Honesty is the best policy.

NO!

Helvétius – Madame Helvétius was one of Ben's closest friends when he was in France. She had eighteen cats and ten dogs. Ben liked her so much, he asked her to marry him, but she said no.

THE COLONIES

I is for *Invention*

Ben Franklin invented all sorts of things. A wind-powered meat roaster. An automatic device to shoo away flies. A claw on a pole for retrieving items from high shelves. A wooden chair that turned into a stepladder when the seat was flipped up.

Industry need not wish.

Indian – In December 1763, a group of angry Pennsylvanians attacked and killed a half-dozen Conestoga Indians. Two weeks later, they killed an even larger number of Conestogas. Then, in February, they headed to Philadelphia to slaughter a large number of Indians who had taken shelter there. Benjamin Franklin was horrified. With only three men at his side, he rode out to meet the advancing mob. It was a tense scene, but Ben managed to reason with the men and, at last, they gave up their plan. More than a hundred lives were saved that day.

Anger is never without reason, but seldom with a good one.

J is for *James*

James Franklin was Ben's older brother, and he taught Ben the printing business. After five years of arguments and misunderstandings, Ben broke his contract and ran away, first to New York, then to Philadelphia.

Later, when Ben returned to Boston for a short visit, James gave him the cold shoulder. It would be years before they made up.

Josiah – Josiah Franklin was Benjamin's father. Born in England, he came to America in 1683, settling in Boston. He earned his living as a candle-maker and soap-maker.

Junto – A young men's club that Ben Franklin started in Philadelphia. Once a week, its members would get together for an evening of spirited conversation.

Jelly – When Ben was old and in poor health, he often dosed himself with a spoonful of blackberry jelly. It made him feel better, he said.

K is for *Key* and *Kite*

In an experiment that made him famous, Ben used a key, a kite, and a foot-long piece of wire to prove that lightning and electricity are the same thing.

Ben's twenty-one-year-old son, William, was with him that stormy day.

Keimer – A printer in Philadelphia, Samuel Keimer was one of Ben's first bosses. But the two didn't get along, and finally Ben quit. Later, Keimer sold his newspaper, the *Gazette*, to Ben.

King – During his long life, Ben stood before five kings: George II and George III of England, Louis XV and Louis XVI of France, and Christian VII of Denmark. He even had lunch with King Christian. To prove it, he drew a diagram of the table, showing where everyone had sat.

Eat to live, and not live to eat.

L is for *Library*

Ben loved reading so much that he started the first subscription library in America. For a small fee, people could borrow books and take them home to read.

Being ignorant is not so much a shame, as being unwilling to learn.

Lion – Ben believed it was important to save money. But when the first lion was exhibited in America, he paid six pennies to see it. It was worth it, he said.

London – Ben Franklin spent a number of years in London, working to protect the interests of Pennsylvania. He spent so much time in London, and made so many friends there, that he worried he was losing touch with the colonies.

I am a strong believer in luck and I find the harder I work the more I have of it.

M is for *Money*

Ben Franklin printed money for the colonies of Pennsylvania, Delaware, and New Jersey. He also printed government documents and treaties.

Memoirs – Ben spent many years writing his memoirs. *The Autobiography of Benjamin Franklin* is still in print today.

Market Street – Ben's three-story brick home in Philadelphia was located on Market Street. A large and comfortable house, it was usually full of visitors. Ben liked having company: His dining table could seat twenty-four.

Remember that time is money.

If you would know the value of money, go try to borrow some.

Little strokes fell great oaks.

N is for *Newspaper*

The finest newspaper in the colonies was Ben Franklin's *Pennsylvania Gazette*. Ben said he wanted his paper to be "agreeable and useful" to its readers. It was.

New-England Courant – James Franklin's newspaper in colonial Boston. Some of Ben's earliest (and funniest) writing appeared in the pages of the *New-England Courant*.

Nude – Every morning, wherever he happened to be, Ben Franklin would take an "air bath." He believed that it was healthy to spend part of each day in the nude. To his regret, "air baths" never caught on in colonial America.

To succeed, jump as quickly at opportunities as you do at conclusions.

Navigation – Ben loved ships. He was constantly studying them, trying to figure out how to make them go faster. He also drew diagrams for new types of anchors.

O is for *Ocean*

Though Ben Franklin crossed the Atlantic numerous times, he never lost his fascination for the sea. To better understand the ocean, he studied currents, wind direction, water and air temperatures, and plant and animal life. The movements of the Gulf Stream were of particular interest to him.

Old South Church – Ben's parents worshiped at Old South Church in Boston. They were Congregationalists, and were constantly encouraging Ben to go to church.

Order – "Let all your things have their places," Ben was fond of saying. But he never managed to bring order into his own life. His desk was always a mess. So were his record books.

Overweight – The older Ben grew, the plumper he became. But he refused to let his weight bother him. Jokingly, he would refer to himself as "Dr. Fatsides."

A small leak will sink a great ship.

P is for *Printer*

Ben took pride in his work as a printer. He kept his presses in good working order, and he used high-quality paper and ink. He wanted his newspapers and almanacs to look good. He also strove to make them easy to read, relying, for instance, on black ink, not gray, which he found too dim. Unfortunately, most printers in the colonies did not set their standards as high as he did. The newspapers in Boston, for instance, tended to be smudgy and difficult to read. According to Ben, if you wanted to keep something a secret, have it printed in a Boston newspaper.

Picnic – Soon after he began experimenting with electricity, Ben hosted a picnic for his friends—an "electric picnic." Every aspect of the day, from food to fun, involved some form of electricity.

Pigeon – Ben Franklin kept pigeons.

Postmaster – As postmaster of Philadelphia, it was Ben's job to get the mail through. He was constantly looking for ways to speed up delivery.

SORRY

If all printers were determined not to print anything till they were sure it would offend nobody, there would be very little printed.

Q is for *Quaker*

There was never a good war or a bad peace.

In the 1700s, Philadelphia was a Quaker town.

A sober-minded and practical people, Quakers spoke out against slavery, refused to bear arms, and believed that men and women should be treated as equals. They also had strong religious beliefs, for which they were sometimes persecuted in the colonies.

One of Ben's first employers, Thomas Denham, was a Quaker. So was Peter Collinson, the friend who sent Ben the equipment that got him interested in making electrical experiments.

Queen's Street – Where James Franklin's printing shop was located in Boston.

QUEEN'S STREET

Quill – Benjamin Franklin used a feathered quill to write with. He and Deborah sold quills in their general store; they also sold ink and writing paper.

NERAL STORE

PAPER

INK

QUILLS

R is for *Revolutionary War*

The most important public event of Ben Franklin's life was the Revolutionary War, which America fought to free itself from Great Britain. Initially, from his post in London, Ben strongly resisted the idea of going to war. But when at last he realized that conflict was unavoidable, he returned to Philadelphia and became a staunch patriot.

Reading – Reading books was one of the great pleasures of Benjamin Franklin's life. "From a child," he wrote, "I was fond of reading, and all the little money that came into my hands was ever laid out in books."

Resolution – "Resolve to perform what you ought," Ben wrote. "Perform without fail what you resolve." In other words, make up your mind to get things done. Then do them.

Rod – In 1752—the same year he conducted his kite experiment—Ben Franklin invented the lightning rod. Simple devices made of metal, lightning rods are used to this day to prevent buildings from being damaged by lightning.

S is for *Store*

For the first eighteen years of their married life, Ben and Deborah Franklin ran a general store. They offered a wide variety of items: writing materials, almanacs, dictionaries; soap, salve, ointments; codfish, mackerel, chocolate, and spices. Even lottery tickets!

Sally – Ben and Deborah's only daughter. Her real name was Sarah, but everyone called her Sally. From the time she was very young, she enjoyed reading as much as her father. Sally, Ben wrote, "is the greatest lover of her book and school of any child I ever knew." It also pleased Ben that Sally was affectionate, well-behaved, and "industrious with her needle."

Slavery – For many years, Benjamin Franklin owned slaves. Toward the end of his life, however, he spoke out against slavery and served as president of an abolitionist society.

Swim – Ben Franklin was a good swimmer—so good, in fact, that when he was nineteen, he considered opening a swimming school.

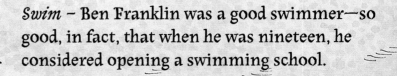

T is for *Treaty*

In 1776, when he was seventy, Ben Franklin sailed to France. His mission: to convince the French government to side with the colonies in the Revolutionary War. It was no easy task, but in the end Ben was successful. The Treaty of Alliance was signed in February 1778.

Temperance – "Eat not to dullness," Ben wrote, "drink not to elevation." Simply put, don't eat too much, don't drink too much. Everything in moderation.

> Nothing more like a fool, than a drunken man.

Tar – During the Revolutionary War, colonists who were suspected of being loyal to King George were often tarred and feathered as punishment.

Turkey – Ben thought the turkey, not the eagle, should be the national bird. Turkeys were respectable, he maintained, whereas eagles were lazy and had a "bad moral character."

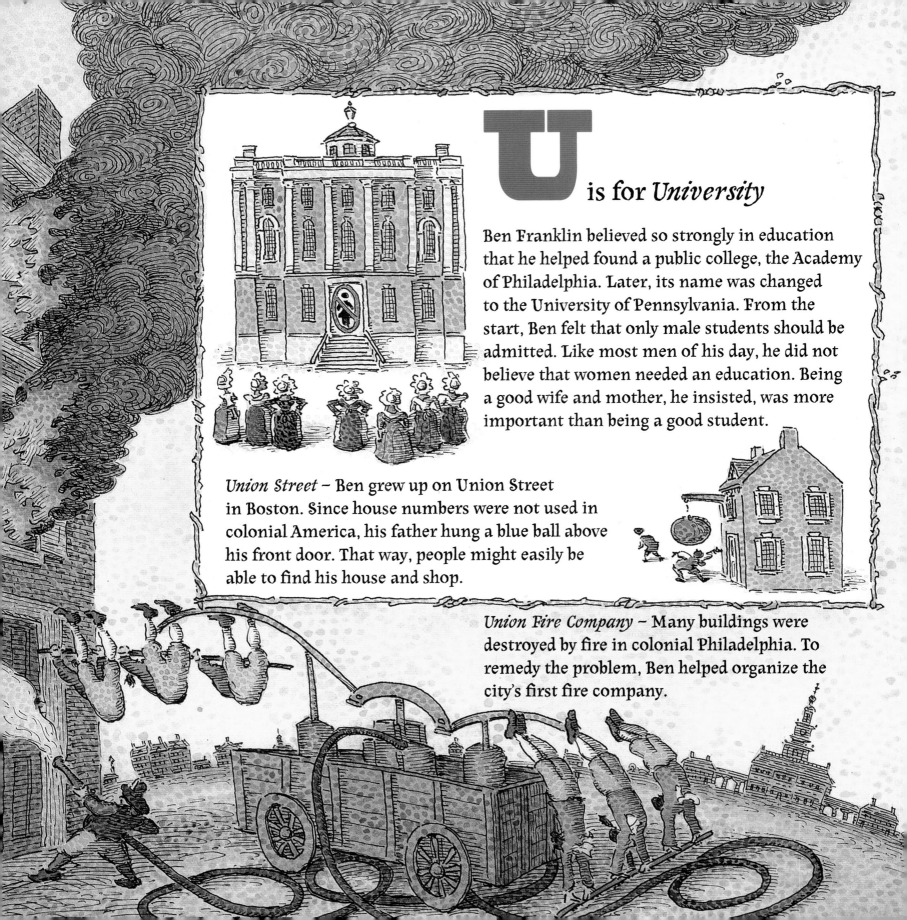

U is for *University*

Ben Franklin believed so strongly in education that he helped found a public college, the Academy of Philadelphia. Later, its name was changed to the University of Pennsylvania. From the start, Ben felt that only male students should be admitted. Like most men of his day, he did not believe that women needed an education. Being a good wife and mother, he insisted, was more important than being a good student.

Union Street – Ben grew up on Union Street in Boston. Since house numbers were not used in colonial America, his father hung a blue ball above his front door. That way, people might easily be able to find his house and shop.

Union Fire Company – Many buildings were destroyed by fire in colonial Philadelphia. To remedy the problem, Ben helped organize the city's first fire company.

Visit your aunt, but not every day;
call at your brother's but not every night.

V is for *Visitors*

Though Benjamin was fond of visitors, even he had his limits. "Fish and visitors smell in three days," he wrote in *Poor Richard's Almanack.*

Vegetarian – When Ben was a teenager, he became a vegetarian—but not for long. He liked eating fish too much.

Valentinois – When Ben Franklin went to France in 1776, he settled at the Hôtel de Valentinois in Passy, a half-hour's drive from Paris. Though he missed his relations in the colonies, he remained in Passy for nearly nine years.

A learned blockhead is a greater blockhead than an ignorant one.

. . . WERE HERE
WISH YOU WERE HERE
WISH YOU WERE HERE
WISH YOU . . .

W is for *William*

William was Ben Franklin's older son. For years, they enjoyed a close relationship, and Ben was extremely pleased when William was appointed royal governor of New Jersey. However, when the Revolutionary War broke out, William's loyalties were to the king, not to the colonies. That caused father and son to have a terrible falling-out. Sadly, they never reconciled.

After the war, William moved to England, where he died in 1813.

Wealth – Like everyone, Ben liked to have money, but he didn't feel the need to be wealthy. Of himself he wrote, "I would rather have it said, *He lived usefully*, than, *He died rich*."

Content makes poor men rich; discontent makes rich men poor.

Washington – George Washington and Benjamin Franklin admired each other greatly. When he died, Ben left his gold-headed walking stick to Washington.

X is for *Xenophon*

When Ben was young, he read a book by the Greek historian Xenophon. It taught him, among other things, the art of persuasion—of getting people to see things in a different way. He studied the book carefully, tried out Xenophon's suggestions, and discovered that they worked. To his delight, he had acquired a new talent.

In time, Ben Franklin became a skilled diplomat, able to persuade rulers of other countries to see—and accept—things from the American point of view.

Xenophile – Benjamin Franklin was a xenophile—that is, he liked foreign people and foreign things. Xenophobes were just the opposite—they disliked anything foreign. Ben didn't understand them.

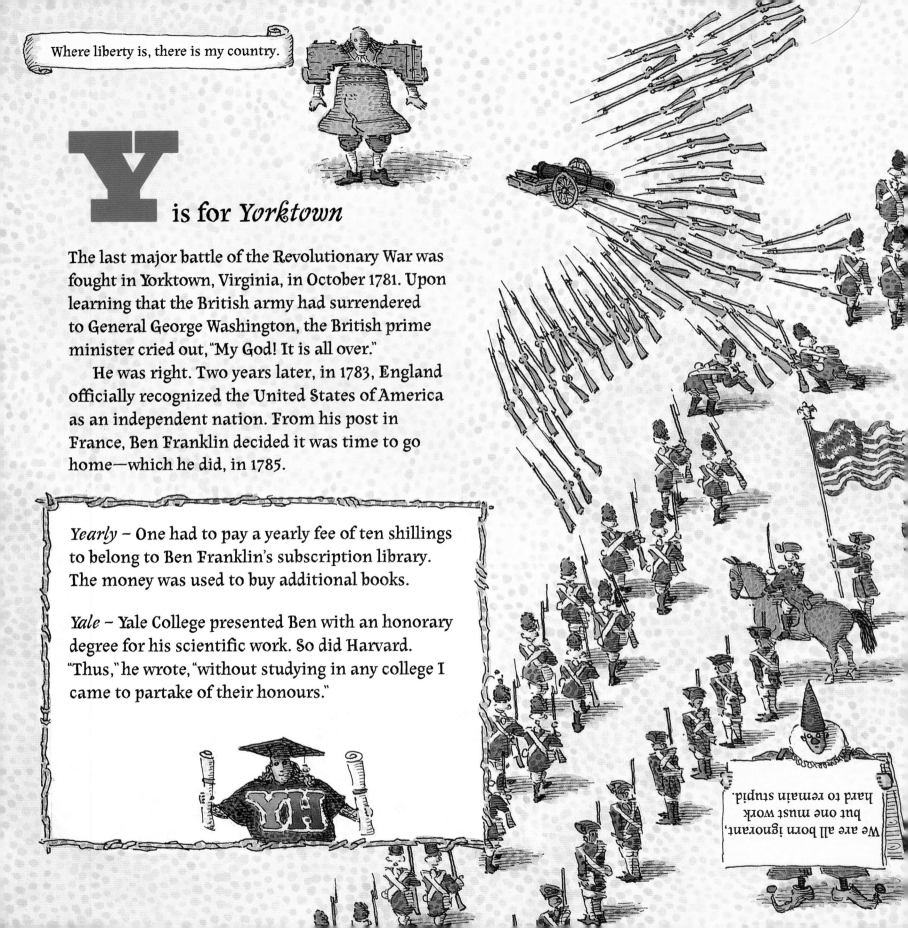

Where liberty is, there is my country.

Y is for *Yorktown*

The last major battle of the Revolutionary War was fought in Yorktown, Virginia, in October 1781. Upon learning that the British army had surrendered to General George Washington, the British prime minister cried out, "My God! It is all over."

He was right. Two years later, in 1783, England officially recognized the United States of America as an independent nation. From his post in France, Ben Franklin decided it was time to go home—which he did, in 1785.

Yearly – One had to pay a yearly fee of ten shillings to belong to Ben Franklin's subscription library. The money was used to buy additional books.

Yale – Yale College presented Ben with an honorary degree for his scientific work. So did Harvard. "Thus," he wrote, "without studying in any college I came to partake of their honours."

We are all born ignorant, but one must work hard to remain stupid.

Energy and persistence conquer all things.

Three may keep a secret, if two of them are dead.

Z is for *Zeal*

From electrical experiments to diplomacy to seeing to it that the streets of Philadelphia were kept clean, Ben approached every project with zeal. Or, as he preferred to call it, "Publick Spirit."

Philadelphia was fortunate to have a son like him. So was the nation.

"Z" – Franklin once wrote a humorous piece, "Petition of the Letter Z," in which Z (or "Zed") complains about being stuck at the end of the alphabet.

And back to A . . .

A is for *American*

Benjamin Franklin was called many things during his life. A patriot. A genius. "A friend to humankind." But he never allowed such praise to go to his head. He wanted, he said, simply to be remembered as "a useful citizen."

Certainly, he got his wish.

Make haste slowly.

An investment in knowledge
always pays the best interest.

For Joe and Jane Purkey, with love
A. S.
For my daughter, Tess
J. O'B.

Text copyright © 2011 by Alan Schroeder
Illustrations copyright © 2011 by John O'Brien
All Rights Reserved
HOLIDAY HOUSE is registered in the U.S. Patent and Trademark Office.
Printed and Bound in October 2011 at Kwong Fat Offset Co., Ltd.,
Dongguan City, Quang Dong Province, China.
The illustrations were done in ink and condensed watercolors
on Strathmore Bristol paper.
The text typeface is Oldavai.
www.holidayhouse.com
3 5 7 9 10 8 6 4 2

Library of Congress Cataloging-in-Publication Data
Schroeder, Alan.
Ben Franklin: his wit and wisdom from A–Z / by Alan Schroeder ;
illustrated by John O'Brien. — 1st ed.
p. cm.
ISBN 978-0-8234-1950-0 (hardcover)
1. Franklin, Benjamin, 1706-1790—Juvenile literature.
2. Statesmen—United States—Biography—Juvenile literature.
3. Inventors—United States—Biography—Juvenile literature.
4. Printers—United States—Biography—Juvenile literature.
5. Alphabet books. I. O'Brien, John, 1953- ill. II. Title.
E302.6.F8S39 2011
973.3092—dc22
[B]
2010024062
ISBN 978-0-8234-2435-1 (paperback)